MY
PR

Edited by Bart Tesoriero
Photography by Kara Hutchinson

Nihil Obstat:	Right Reverend Archimandrite Francis Vivona, S.T.M., J.C.L.
Imprimatur:	Most Reverend Joseph A. Pepe, D.D., J.C.D.
Date:	September 22, 2009

We would like to give special thanks to Father Kenneth Fryar, FSSP, for his encouragement, consultation, and prayer support for this book, as well as for his permission to photograph his celebration of the Mass, and also his server, Dr. Edgardo Aguinaldo. We also thank Father John Ehrich, STL, pastor of Saint Thomas the Apostle parish, Phoenix, Arizona, for his kind permission to photograph the Mass at his parish. Finally we thank Father Brian Austin, FSSP, for his consultation and encouragement.

Library of Congress Control Number: 2012940089
ISBN 1-61796-068-0

Sixth Printing, December, 2019

TABLE OF CONTENTS

INTRODUCTION

Now this is eternal life, that they should know you,
the only true God, and the one whom you sent, Jesus Christ.
—JOHN 17:3

Jesus, Our Lord, Savior, and Brother, reveals God as our Father who wants *all* of His children to be one with Him. God invites us through His Church to share this communion between the Father and the Son in their Spirit of love. The apex of this shared communion is the Holy Sacrifice of the Mass, wherein we celebrate the saving work of Christ's Passion, Death, and Resurrection, receive His Body and Blood, and go forth to love and serve. This mystery of Christ is so incredibly rich that "it cannot be exhausted by its expression in any single Liturgical tradition." (*The Catechism of the Catholic Church*, No. 1201).

In his Motu Proprio *Summorum Pontificum*, issued in 2007, Pope Benedict XVI granted greater freedom to celebrate the traditional Latin Mass, the "extraordinary form" of the Roman Rite, in order to help reconcile "in the heart of the Church" those who "adhered with great love and affection to the earlier liturgical forms." Whether you are returning to the Latin Mass or this is your first time, we hope this book will help you more easily understand and participate in this "ancient treasure" of the Church, that you may more fully experience the presence of Christ through its reverence and sanctity, and thus come to more deeply experience the love of God for you, His dearly beloved child.

How to Use This Book

The Ordinary—the Order—of the Mass, including the parts which remain the same for each Mass, begins on page 18. Our book is structured much like a traditional Missal, with the Latin text on the left side and the English on the right. The parts said by the Priest are marked with a **P.**, and the server's responses are marked with an **S.** Traditionally, the server represents the congregation and hence is the only one who responds out loud in Latin. This practice varies somewhat, so please follow the usage of your particular community.

The rubrics for the Mass—the directives for the actions of the priest and congregation—are printed in red italics. The Propers of the Mass—the parts that change with each Mass—are outlined in a red box, to alert you to turn to the Mass of the day in your Missal for the correct reading or prayer. If you do not have a Missal, either pray silently at this time or look on with another.

The directions of correct posture during Mass—Stand, Kneel, etc.—are printed in black capital letters on the right hand of the page. Again, these directions can vary somewhat with different communities, so please follow local usage.

Most importantly, may God grant to you, and all of us, the grace to participate intensely interiorly in the Mass as we pray along with the priest and our fellow worshippers. Thus may we more fully offer God our adoration, contrition, supplication, and thanksgiving, and receive in return His undying love.

THE HISTORY OF THE MASS

"God, infinitely perfect and blessed in himself, in a plan of sheer goodness freely created man to make him share his own blessed life."
–Paragraph 1, *Catechism of the Catholic Church*

God's original intention to bring all humanity into an eternal communion with Himself remains the same yesterday, today, and forever. After the Fall of our first parents, God promised a Redeemer and made a covenant with Abraham, promising to make of him a great nation, through which all the earth would ultimately be blessed.

In the Passover, God commanded each Hebrew family to sacrifice an unblemished male lamb and to apply its blood on the doorposts and lintel of each house. That night, they must roast the lamb and eat its flesh with unleavened bread. On that very same night the LORD struck down every first born male of Egypt. The blood of the Passover lamb, however, marked the houses of the Israelites; God passed over them, and delivered them from Egypt.

The Lord commanded the Jews to keep the Passover as a memorial feast throughout their generations. God freed Israel from bondage and established a covenant with them, that they might be His people, and that He might be their one and only God. By accepting the covenant, Israel accepted God as their Father, and agreed to share family life with Him.

On the night before He died, Jesus gathered His twelve apostles, and together they came to the upper room to celebrate the Passover. During the meal, Jesus took the bread, gave thanks, blessed it, and then said, "This is my body, which will be given for you; do this in memory of me" (LUKE 22:19).

Jesus then took the large chalice of wine, blessed it, and gave it to His disciples, saying, "Drink from it, all of you, for this is my blood of the covenant, which will be shed on behalf of many for the forgiveness of sins" (MATTHEW 26:27-28).

Jesus thus instituted a new and eternal covenant by changing the Passover bread and wine into His own body and blood. The Church calls this mystery the Transubstantiation. He who would be sacrificed on Calvary shared the covenant meal with His apostles, ushering in a New Covenant with all of us, Jew and Gentile alike. Jesus invited His apostles to enter into a true communion– a sacramental union–with Himself. He commissioned and commanded them to continue celebrating this Eucharist, so named from the Greek *Eucharistia*: Thanksgiving. It was the first Mass, the Holy Sacrifice and the Sacred Meal.

On Good Friday, laden with the sins of the whole world, Jesus died for our sins in obedience to His Father and in accordance with the scriptures. "For our sake he made him to be sin who did not know sin, so that we might become the righteousness of God in him" (2 CORINTHIANS 5:21). Son of God and Son of Man, the humble and obedient Lamb of God offered Himself completely to His Father. God accepted the sacrifice of His Son. The atonement was completed, and satisfaction was made.

In the Eucharist, Jesus makes present again His sacrificial offering of Himself to His Father at Calvary, and His giving of Himself as sacred food so all can commune with Him. This inestimable gift makes present Christ's death and Resurrection

By 150 AD, the basic structure of the Eucharist was in place. Saint Justin Martyr tells us that Mass was celebrated on Sundays; it was "the Flesh and Blood of Jesus Incarnate," to which the community gave their assent with their "Amen." The Mass included two readings, a homily, a procession of gifts, a collection for the poor, the Eucharistic Prayer, and the distribution of Communion.

As Christianity came to be accepted in the empire, Constantine built basilicas–large churches modeled on the Roman public halls–for the Christians to use. Saint Ambrose of Milan and others composed hymns such as the magnificent hymn, *Te Deum,* so everyone could honor God together. The worshippers sang the *Gloria*, *Sanctus*, and the *Agnus Dei*.

With the introduction of basilicas, bishops, priests, and deacons wore more formal clothing, handed down to us as the vestments of the Mass. The readings of the Mass were taken from the Old and New Testaments. The celebrant "broke open" the Word in his homily, so Christ could be received both at the table of the Word and in His presence *par excellence* at the table of the Eucharist. All of this was focused on one overarching theme: The Body of Christ in the Eucharist—*corpus mysticum*, according to the Fathers of the Church—makes the Body of Christ—*corpus verum*—which is the Church. The Eucharist is given to transform *us* into the Body of Christ!

In 1545, Pope Paul III convened the Council of Trent to clarify Catholic doctrine on salvation, sacraments, Scripture, and Tradition. The Council standardized the Mass, decreeing a uniformity followed by the Church for centuries. In 1570, Pope Saint Pius V produced the Roman Missal—the standard for the Roman Rite.

The priest would be the celebrant, the acolytes would represent the community, and the people would participate more interiorly in the Holy Sacrifice of the Mass. Everything, including the readings, was to be read in Latin. The Council of Trent restated the eternal truths of the liturgy, and gave to the faithful an ordered, true presentation of the Mass. Since the liturgy is living, after four centuries the Church needed the Holy Spirit to breathe upon her children, renewing their faith and helping them celebrate the Eucharist in new and life-giving ways, while not discarding the beauty and reverence of the old.

The seeds of the liturgical renewal sprouted in the mid-19th century, with the revival of Gregorian chant and studies of liturgical history under the inspiration of the French Benedictine abbot Dom Guéranger. In 1909, an international conference on the liturgy stressed the need for active participation of the laity in the Mass. Father Romano Guardini and others urged Catholics to see beyond the externals of the liturgy, beautiful as they were, to encounter the Lord waiting to meet us. In his encyclical *Mediator Dei,* Pope Pius XII called for the community to have the true spirit of the liturgy, to realize and reverence the Real Presence of Christ in the Eucharist.

In the pivotal document *Sacrosanctum Concilium*–The Constitution on the Sacred Liturgy–issued in 1963, the Vatican II Council Fathers emphasized that the Eucharist is the source and summit of our lives. They called all worshippers to a full, conscious, and active participation, "which is demanded by the very nature of the liturgy." We gain our "true Christian spirit" primarily and indispensably from the sacred liturgy, "and therefore pastors of souls must zealously strive to achieve it."

The Mass of Pope Paul VI is today the ordinary or normal form of the Roman Rite Mass. This Mass retains the essential structure of the Tridentine Mass, while eliminating elements such as the prayers at the foot of the altar, the silent praying of the Canon, and the "Last Gospel" at the end of Mass. Mass is now offered in the vernacular, the treasury of Sacred Scripture is opened more fully, and the faithful are invited to participate more fully in the liturgy.

Pope Benedict XVI, as a seminarian, studied Father Guardini's seminal work, *The Spirit of the Liturgy*. He wrote that Guardini's book "helped us to rediscover the liturgy in all its beauty, hidden wealth, and time-transcending grandeur...." It motivated him, and others, to seek for a more "substantial" celebration of the liturgy as the prayer of the Church, inspired and directed by the Holy Spirit himself, "a prayer in which Christ unceasingly becomes contemporary with us, enters into our lives."

After his election as pope in 2005, the Holy Father issued the Motu Proprio– "on his own initiative"– *Summorum Pontificum*, liberalizing the use of the 1962 Roman Missal. He reiterated that the ordinary liturgy of the Roman Church was the one promulgated by Pope Paul VI, commonly used today. He stated, however, that the Roman Missal promulgated by Pope Saint Pius V and re-issued by Saint Pope John XXIII–the Tridentine Mass–is to be considered an extraordinary expression, or form, of the liturgy. Pope Benedict allowed all priests to celebrate that traditional Latin Mass. Priests could use either Missal and administer the sacraments in their pre-Vatican II format without needing permission from the local bishop.

Pope Benedict wanted to help Traditionalist Catholics to reconcile "in the heart of the Church." He also wanted other Catholics to have an opportunity to experience the Latin Mass, through which, for centuries, the Lord has nourished the spiritual life of many saints, built up His presence in the hearts of His people, and "fecundated"–enriched–"their piety."

A BRIEF GUIDE TO THE LATIN MASS

The Extraordinary form of the Roman Rite–the traditional Latin Mass–is divided into two parts: The Mass of the Catechumens and the Mass of the Faithful. *Catechumens* is Greek for those people who are being given catechesis–formal instruction in the Catholic Faith–in preparation for Baptism and full participation in the sacramental life of the Church.

Every Mass is made up of the Ordinary, or unchangeable parts, of the Mass, and Propers–changeable parts–such as the specific prayers. There is a one-year cycle of Scripture readings, which the Priest typically proclaims in Latin. You will need to use a Missal to read the Propers and the Readings for each Mass.

A Solemn High Mass is celebrated with deacon and subdeacon, chant, and incense. It is a beautiful and reverent gift of praise to God. Space does not permit us to include Solemn Mass rubrics in our book at this time. Instead, we are featuring a Low Mass, which is a more common form of the liturgy.

The celebrant faces the altar for the entire Mass, turning only a few times to the assembly. The Mass begins with prayers from Psalm 42 and the *Confiteor*, prayed at the foot of the altar, as the priest and people ask God's forgiveness and mercy before ascending, as it were, to Mount Calvary for the Holy Sacrifice of the Cross. The celebrant prays the *Introit* (Latin for "He enters") prayer, one of the Propers of the Mass, followed by the *Kyrie Eleison* (Greek for "Lord, have mercy").

On Sundays and Feast days, the priest prays the *Gloria*, the Church's greatest hymn of praise, first composed in Greek. He continues by praying the *Prayer*, or *Collect*, of the day, collecting, as it were, the people and their intentions and bringing them to the Lord.

The celebrant then reads the *Epistle*, followed by the *Gradual*, a time-honored Psalm response to God's Word. The *Alleluia* (or *Tract*, in Penitential seasons) follows as a prelude to the *Gospel*. The server moves the altar missal from the Epistle side to the Gospel side of the altar, an early custom of proclaiming the Gospel northwards, towards the pagan barbarians. On Sundays and certain feast days, the *Creed* is recited after the Gospel. Afterwards, the Catechumens would be dismissed.

The priest begins the Mass of the Faithful, praying the Offertory verse. He offers the host to God. He then pours wine and a little water into the chalice, praying that just as Jesus humbled Himself to partake of our humanity, we might be made worthy to share in His divinity.

The celebrant washes his hands, symbolizing his desire for purity as he prepares to offer the sacrifice to the Most High God. He asks the Holy Trinity to accept this oblation, and then, in the *Orate Fratres*, implores the congregation to pray with him. The priest then silently prays the *Secret*, and we come to the *Preface* of the Canon of the Mass.

The *Preface* is a hymn of thanksgiving and praise for the many gifts God has given us, especially for the gift of His Son for our salvation. The celebrant exhorts us to not only praise God but in fact to dismiss all earthly cares and spiritually to enter heaven, where we join the Divine Liturgy already in process.

All of this builds up to the *Sanctus*, (Latin for *Holy*), repeated three times, in praise of Almighty God. *Hosanna* is the Hebrew for "Grant salvation!" from Psalm 117, and we proclaim it with praise and joy. We kneel now, helping us to concentrate more intently and reverently, as the priest continues. The Tridentine Mass has one Eucharistic Prayer or Canon (the Roman Canon)–dating back to the first centuries of the Church–which the priest prays in reverent silence.

The server rings the bell as the priest extends his hands, asking God to accept and bless our gifts that they might become the Body and Blood of His Son. The celebrant then says the words of *Consecration*, the most solemn moment of the Mass. God, speaking through His priest, transubstantiates the bread and wine into the Body and Blood, Soul and Divinity of Jesus Christ.

After the Consecration, the priest offers the Victim to God, asking Him to accept our gift and to bless us in return. He then prays for the dead, and for all of us as well. In the Minor Elevation the celebrant offers all creation back to God through Christ, as the Canon ends in a burst of praise: All glory to God!

We now prepare to commune with Our Lord by praying the *Pater Noster*—the Our Father—followed by an ancient prayer for deliverance from all evil. We then have the breaking of the Sacred Host, a sign of Jesus' being broken for us and for our salvation. The priest prays that the peace of the Lord may be always with us, and in our name the server extends this blessed peace back to the priest. The priest drops a small particle of the Sacred Host into the chalice. This commingling symbolizes the Resurrection, as the Body and Blood of Christ are symbolically rejoined. The celebrant continues by praying the *Agnus Dei*—Lamb of God—for forgiveness and peace.

The priest receives Holy Communion and we prepare ourselves. The servers pray the *Confiteor* in the name of the congregation, and then three times the priest prays for us, *Domine non sum dignus*—"Lord, I am not worthy, that You should come under my roof; only say the word and my soul will be healed."

The faithful receive Holy Communion kneeling and on the tongue. The priest then offers prayers of thanksgiving as he cleanses the chalice. He prays the Communion and Postcommunion prayer, and says, "Ite, Missa est."—"Go, you are sent forth." The priest then gives us the final blessing, followed by the Last Gospel, which is taken from the first chapter of the Gospel of Saint John. The Last Gospel is a profound reflection on the gift of Christ Jesus to us, and of our invited response. We end with *Deo Gratias*—"Thanks be to God for his unspeakable gift!" (2 CORINTHIANS 9:15).

PRAYERS BEFORE MASS

Prayer Before Mass

By Saint Thomas Aquinas

ALMIGHTY and ever-lasting God, I approach the sacrament of Thy only-begotten Son, our Lord Jesus Christ. I come sick to the doctor of life, unclean to the fountain of mercy, blind to the radiance of eternal light, and poor and needy to the Lord of heaven and earth. Therefore, I implore Thee in Thy great generosity, to heal my sickness, wash away my defilement, enlighten my blindness, enrich my poverty, and clothe my nakedness, so that I may receive the Bread of angels, the King of kings, and the Lord of lords with reverence and humility, with contrition and devotion, with purity and faith, and with such purpose and determination that will be expedient to the salvation of my soul. Grant me, I beseech Thee, that I may not only receive the Sacrament of the Body and Blood of the Lord, but also the reality and power of the Sacrament. O most kind God, grant that I may receive the Body of Thine only-begotten Son, our Lord Jesus Christ, born of the Virgin Mary, and so received that I may be worthy to be incorporated into His mystical body, and numbered among His members. O most loving Father, grant me Thy beloved Son, which I now receive under the veil of a sacrament, that I may one day behold Him face to face in glory, Who lives and reigns with Thee in the unity of the Holy Spirit, God, forever. Amen.

Prayer to the Blessed Virgin Mary

O Mother of mercy and of love, most blessed Virgin Mary, I a poor and unworthy sinner, fly to you with all my heart and all my affection. I implore your loving kindness, that even as you stood beside your dearly beloved Son as He hung upon the cross, so please also stand by me, a sinner; by the priest who is offering Mass here today; and beside all your faithful people receiving the most sacred Body of your Son. Grant that, aided by your help, we may offer a worthy and acceptable sacrifice in the sight of the most high and undivided Trinity. Amen.

Prayer to Saint Joseph

O Blessed Joseph, happy man, to whom it was given not only to see and to hear that God whom many kings longed to see, yet saw not, to hear, yet heard not; but also to carry Him in your arms and to kiss Him, to clothe Him and to watch over him:

V. Pray for us, blessed Joseph.
R. That we may be made worthy of the promises of Christ.

Let us pray. O God, Who has given us a royal priesthood, we pray to you that, as Blessed Joseph was found worthy to touch with his hands and to hold in his arms Your only begotten Son, born of the Virgin Mary, so may we be made fit, by cleanness of heart and blamelessness of life, to minister at Your holy altar; may we with reverent devotion partake of the Sacred Body and Blood of Your Son, and may we in the world to come be accounted worthy of receiving an everlasting reward. Through the same Christ our Lord. Amen.

THE ORDINARY OF THE MASS

I. MASS OF THE CATECHUMENS

BEGINNING OF MASS

The Priest (P.) and Server (S.) enter the Sanctuary. They genuflect, make the Sign of the Cross, and pray at the foot of the Altar:

KNEEL

P. IN nomine Patris, ✠ et Fílii, et Spíritus Sancti. Amen.

P. Introíbo ad altáre Dei.

S. *Ad Deum qui lætíficat iuventútem meam.*

THE ORDINARY OF THE MASS

I. MASS OF THE CATECHUMENS

In the Mass, the servers represent the congregation. Therefore they respond audibly to the Priest, while you are invited to pray silently, yet attentively, as you enter these Sacred Mysteries at God's personal invitation to you:

All you who are thirsty,
come to the water!
You who have no money,
come, receive grain and eat;
Come, without paying and without cost,
drink wine and milk!

ISAIAH 55:1

BEGINNING OF MASS

The Priest **(P.)** *and Server* **(S.)** *enter the Sanctuary. They genuflect, make the Sign of the Cross, and pray at the foot of the Altar:*

KNEEL

P. IN THE NAME of the Father, ✠ and of the Son, and of the Holy Spirit. Amen.

P. I will go in unto the Altar of God.

S. To God, Who gives joy to my youth.

Psalm 42

P. JÚDICA me, Deus, et discérne cáusam meam de gente non sancta: ab hómine iníquo et dolóso érue me.

S. *Quia tu es, Deus, fortitúdo mea: quare me repulísti, et quare tristis incédo, dum afflígit me inimícus?*

P. Emítte lucem tuam et veritátem tuam: ipsa me deduxérunt et adduxérunt in montem sanctum tuum, et in tabernácula tua.

S. *Et introíbo ad altáre Dei: ad Deum qui lætíficat iuventútem meam.*

P. Confitébor tibi in cíthara, Deus, Deus meus: quare tristis es anima mea, et quare contúrbas me?

S. *Spera in Deo, quóniam adhuc confitébor illi: salutáre vultus mei, et Deus meus.*

P. Glória Patri, et Filio, et Spirítui Sancto.

S. *Sicut erat in princípio, et nunc, et semper: et in sæcula sæculórum. Amen.*

P. Introíbo ad altáre Dei.

S. *Ad Deum qui lætíficat iuventútem meam.*

Psalm 42

P. JUDGE me, O God, and distinguish my cause from the nation that is not holy: deliver me from the unjust and deceitful man.

S. For Thou, O God, art my strength: why hast Thou cast me off? and why do I go sorrowful while the enemy afflicts me?

P. Send forth Thy light and Thy truth: they have led me and brought me unto Thy holy hill, and into Thy tabernacles.

S. And I will go in unto the Altar of God: unto God, Who gives joy to my youth.

P. I will praise Thee upon the harp, O God, my God: why art thou sad, O my soul? and why do thou disquiet me?

S. Hope thou in God, for I will yet praise Him: Who is the salvation of my countenance, and my God.

P. Glory be to the Father, and to the Son, and to the Holy Spirit.

S. As it was in the beginning, is now, and ever shall be, world without end. Amen.

P. I will go in unto the Altar of God.

S. To God, Who gives joy to my youth.

P. Adjutórium nostrum ✠ in nómine Dómini.

S. *Qui fecit cælum et terram.*

The Priest bows down and prays the Confiteor.

P. Confíteor Deo, etc.

S. *Misereátur tui omnípotens Deus, et dimissis peccátis tuis, perdúcat te ad vitam ætérnam.*

P. Amen.

The Server then bows and prays the Confiteor.

Confíteor Deo omnipoténti, beátæ Maríæ semper Vírgini, beáto Michaéli Archángelo, beáto Joánni Baptístæ, sanctis Apóstolis Petro et Páulo, ómnibus Sanctis, et tibi, Pater: quia peccávi nimis cogitatióne, verbo, et ópere: (stike breast three times) mea culpa, mea culpa, mea máxima culpa. Ideo precor beátam Maríam semper Virginem, beátum Michaélem Archángelum, beátum Joánnem Baptístam, sanctos Apóstolos Petrum et Páulum, omnes Sanctos, et te, Pater, oráre pro me ad Dóminum Deum nostrum.

P. Misereátur vestri omnípotens Deus, et dimíssis peccátis vestris, perdúcat vos ad vitam æternam.

S. *Amen.*

P. Our help ✠ is in the Name of the Lord.

S. Who has made heaven and earth.

The Priest bows down and prays the Confiteor.

P. I confess to almighty God, etc.

S. May Almighty God have mercy upon you, forgive you your sins, and bring you to life everlasting.

P. Amen.

We pray the Confiteor silently:

I confess to Almighty God, to blessed Mary ever Virgin, to blessed Michael the Archangel, to blessed John the Baptist, to the holy Apostles Peter and Paul, to all the Saints, and to you, Father, that I have sinned exceedingly, in thought, word and deed: *(stike breast three times)* through my fault, through my fault, through my most grievous fault. Therefore I beseech blessed Mary ever Virgin, blessed Michael the Archangel, blessed John the Baptist, the holy Apostles Peter and Paul, all the Saints, and you Father, to pray to the Lord our God for me.

P. May Almighty God have mercy upon you, forgive you your sins, and bring you to life everlasting.

S. Amen.

The Priest makes the sign of the cross, praying:

P. Indulgéntiam, ✠ absolutiónem, et remissiónem peccatórum nostrórum, tríbuat nobis omnípotens et misericors Dóminus.

S. *Amen.*

P. Deus, tu convérsus vivificábis nos.

S. *Et plebs tua lætábitur in te.*

P. Osténde nobis Dómine, misericórdiam tuam.

S. *Et salutáre tuum da nobis.*

P. Dómine, exáudi oratiónem meam.

S. *Et clamor meus ad te véniat.*

P. Dóminus vobíscum.

S. *Et cum spíritu tuo.*

P. Orémus.

Going up the Altar, the Priest prays silently:

Aufer a nobis, quaesumus, Dómine, iniquitátes nostras: ut ad Sancta sanctórum puris mereámur méntibus introíre. Per Christum Dóminum nostrum. Amen.

The Priest makes the sign of the cross, praying:

P. May the Almighty and merciful God grant us pardon, ✠ absolution, and remission of our sins.

S. Amen.

P. Thou wilt turn, O God, and bring us to life.

S. And Thy people shall rejoice in Thee.

P. Show us, O Lord, Thy mercy.

S. And grant us Thy salvation.

P. O Lord, hear my prayer.

S. And let my cry come unto Thee.

P. The Lord be with you.

S. And with thy spirit.

P. Let us pray.

Going up the Altar, the Priest prays silently:

Take away from us our iniquities, we entreat Thee, O Lord, that with pure minds we may worthily enter into the Holy of Holies. Through Christ our Lord. Amen.

Bowing down, the Priest kisses the Altar, and prays:

Orámus te, Dómine, per mérita Sanctórum tuórum, quorum relíquiæ hic sunt, et ómnium Sanctórum: ut indúlgere dignéris ómnia peccáta mea. Amen.

Standing at the Epistle side of the Altar, the Priest reads the Introit, which is a Proper of the Mass, and therefore varies daily.

THE INTROIT

(Turn to appropriate Missal page)

THE KYRIE

P. KYRIE eléison.

S. Kýrie eléison.

P. Kýrie eléison.

S. Christe eléison.

P. Christe eléison.

S. Christe eléison.

P. Kýrie eléison.

S. Kýrie eléison.

P. Kýrie eléison.

Bowing down, the Priest kisses the Altar, and prays:

We beseech Thee, O Lord, by the merits of Thy Saints, whose relics are here, and of all the Saints, that Thou wilt deign to pardon me all my sins. Amen.

Standing at the Epistle side of the Altar, the Priest reads the Introit, which is a Proper of the Mass, and therefore varies daily.

THE INTROIT

(Turn to appropriate Missal page)

THE KYRIE

P. LORD, have mercy on us.

S. Lord, have mercy on us.

P. Lord, have mercy on us.

S. Christ, have mercy on us.

P. Christ, have mercy on us.

S. Christ, have mercy on us.

P. Lord, have mercy on us.

S. Lord, have mercy on us.

P. Lord, have mercy on us.

THE GLORIA

The Priest stands at the middle of the Altar, and prays the Gloria.

GLORIA in excélsis Deo, et in terra pax homínibus bonæ voluntátis. Laudámus te. Benedícimus te. Adorámus te. Glorificámus te. Grátias ágimus tibi propter magnam glóriam tuam. Dómine Deus, Rex cœléstis, Deus Pater omnípotens. Dómine Fili unigénite, Jesu Christe. Dómine Deus, Agnus Dei, Fílius Patris. Qui tollis peccáta mundi, miserére nobis. Qui tollis peccáta mundi, súscipe deprecatiónem nostram. Qui sedes ad déxteram Patris, miserére nobis. Quóniam tu solus Sanctus. Tu solus Dóminus. Tu solus Altíssimus, Jesu Christe. Cum Sancto Spíritu ✠ in glória Dei Patris. Amen.

Turning to the people, the Priest says:

P. Dóminus vobíscum.

S. *Et cum spíritu tuo.*

P. Orémus.

THE PRAYER

(Turn to appropriate Missal page)

The Priest prays the Prayer for this day.

P. Per ómnia sæcula sæculórum.

S. *Amen.*

THE GLORIA

The Priest stands at the middle of the Altar, and prays the Gloria.

GLORY be to God on high. And on earth peace to men of good will. We praise Thee. We bless Thee. We adore Thee. We glorify Thee. We give Thee thanks for Thy great glory. O Lord God, heavenly King, God the Father Almighty. O Lord Jesus Christ, Only-begotten Son. O Lord God, Lamb of God, Son of the Father. Who takes away the sins of the world, have mercy on us. Who takes away the sins of the world, receive our prayer. Who sits at the right hand of the Father, have mercy on us. For Thou alone art holy. Thou alone art the Lord. Thou alone, O Jesus Christ, art most high. With the Holy Spirit, ✠ in the glory of God the Father. Amen.

Turning to the people, the Priest says:

P. The Lord be with you.

S. And with thy spirit.

P. Let us pray.

THE PRAYER

(Turn to appropriate Missal page)

The Priest prays the Prayer for this day.

P. World without end.

S. Amen.

THE EPISTLE

SIT

(Turn to appropriate Missal page)

The Priest reads the Epistle from the Mass he is celebrating.

S. *Deo Gratias.*

The Priest then reads the Gradual and Alleluia or Tract.
He returns to the middle of the Altar, bows, and prays:

Munda cor meum ac lábia mea, omnípotens Deus, qui lábia Isaíæ Prophétæ cálculo mundásti ignito: ita me tua grata miseratióne dignáre mundáre, ut sanctum Evangélium tuum digne váleam nuntiáre. Per Christum Dóminum nostrum. Amen.

Jube, Dómine, benedícere.
Dóminus sit in corde meo et in lábiis meis: ut digne et competénter annúntiem Evangélium suum. Amen.

THE GOSPEL

STAND

(Turn to appropriate Missal page)

The Priest goes to the Gospel side of the Altar
and proclaims the Holy Gospel from the Mass of the day.

P. Dóminus vobíscum.

S. *Et cum spíritu tuo.*

P. ✠ Sequéntia (Inítium) Sancti Evangélii secúndum N.,

S. *Glória tibi, Dómine.*

THE EPISTLE

SIT

(Turn to appropriate Missal page)

The Priest reads the Epistle from the Mass he is celebrating. At the end:

S. *Thanks be to God.*

The Priest then reads the Gradual and Alleluia or Tract. He returns to the middle of the Altar, bows, and prays:

Cleanse my heart and my lips, O Almighty God, Who cleansed the lips of the prophet Isaias with a burning coal; through Thy gracious mercy so purify me that I may worthily proclaim Thy holy Gospel. Through Christ our Lord. Amen.

Grant, O Lord, Thy blessing.
May the Lord be in my heart and on my lips, that I may worthily and fittingly proclaim His Gospel. Amen.

THE GOSPEL

STAND

(Turn to appropriate Missal page)

P. The Lord be with you.

S. And with thy spirit.

P. ✠ The continuation (or The beginning) of the holy Gospel according to Saint *N.*

S. Glory be to Thee, O Lord.

The Priest then reads the Gospel of the day.

S. *Laus tibi, Christe.*

The Priest kisses the Gospel, and says:

P. Per evangelica dicta deleantur nostra delicta.

THE CREDO (NICENE CREED)

CREDO in unum Deum, Patrem omnipoténtem, factórem coeli et terræ, visibílium ómnium et invisibílium. Et in unum Dóminum Jesum Christum, Fílium Dei unigénitum. Et ex Patre natum ante ómnia sæcula. Deum de Deo, lumen de lúmine, Deum verum de Deo vero. Génitum, non factum, consubstantiálem Patri: per quem ómnia facta sunt.

Qui propter nos hómines, et propter nostram salútem descéndit de cœlis. *(Here genuflect.)* Et incarnátus est de Spíritu Sancto ex María Vírgine: **ET HOMO FACTUS EST** *(Rise.)*

The Priest then reads the Gospel of the day.

S. Praise be to Thee, O Christ.

The Priest kisses the Gospel, and says:

P. By the words of the Gospel may our sins be blotted out.

THE CREDO (NICENE CREED)

I Believe in one God, the Father Almighty, Maker of heaven and earth, and of all things visible and invisible. And in one Lord Jesus Christ, the Only-begotten Son of God, born of the Father before all ages; God of God, Light of Light, true God of true God; Begotten, not made: consubstantial with the Father, by Whom all things were made. Who for us men, and for our salvation, came down from heaven. *(Here genuflect.)* And was incarnate by the Holy Spirit of the Virgin Mary: **AND WAS MADE MAN.** *(Rise.)*

Crucifíxus etiam pro nobis; sub Póntio Pilato passus, et sepúltus est. Et resurréxit tértia die, secúndum Scripturas. Et ascéndit in coelum: sedet ad déxteram Patris. Et íterum ventúrus est cum glória judicáre vivos et mórtuos: cujus regni non erit finis. Et in Spíritum Sanctum, Dóminum et vivificántem: qui ex Patre Filióque procédit. Qui cum Patre et Filio simul adorátur, et conglorificátur: qui locútus est per Prophétas. Et unam, sanctam, catholicam et apostólicam Ecclésiam. Confíteor unum baptísma in remissiónem peccatórum. Et exspécto resurrectiónem mortuórum. Et vitam ✠ ventúri sæculi. Amen.

II. MASS OF THE FAITHFUL

The Priest turns toward the people and prays:

P. Dóminus vobíscum.

S. *Et cum spíritu tuo.*

P. Orémus.

THE OFFERTORY

SIT

(Turn to appropriate Missal page for the Offertory Verse)

The Priest prays the Offertory Verse. Then he uncovers the chalice, places the host on the paten and offers it to God:

Offering of the Host

He was crucified also for us, suffered under Pontius Pilate, and was buried. And on the third day He rose again, according to the Scriptures, and He ascended into heaven. He sits at the right hand of the Father: and He shall come again with glory, to judge the living and the dead: and His kingdom shall have no end. And in the Holy Spirit, the Lord and Giver of Life, Who proceeds from the Father and the Son, Who, together with the Father and the Son, is adored and glorified: Who spoke through the Prophets. And in One, Holy, Catholic and Apostolic Church. I confess one Baptism for the remission of sins. And I look for the resurrection of the dead, and the life ✠ of the world to come. Amen.

II. MASS OF THE FAITHFUL

The Priest turns toward the people and prays:

P. The Lord be with you.

S. And with thy spirit.

P. Let us pray.

THE OFFERTORY

SIT

(Turn to appropriate Missal page for the Offertory Verse)

The Priest prays the Offertory Verse. Then he uncovers the chalice, places the host on the paten and offers it to God:

Offering of the Host

SÚSCIPE, sancte Pater, omnípotens ætérne Deus, hanc immaculátam hóstiam, quam ego indígnus fámulus tuus óffero tibi, Deo meo vivo et vero, pro innumerabílibus peccátis, et offensiónibus, et negligéntiis meis, et pro ómnibus circumstántibus, sed et pro ómnibus fidélibus Christiánis vivis atque defúnctis: ut mihi, et illis profíciat ad salútem in vitam ætérnam. Amen.

Offering of the Chalice

Making the Sign of the Cross with the paten, the priest places the host upon the corporal. He pours wine and water into the chalice, blessing the water before it is mixed, in remembrance of the water and blood which flowed from the side of Jesus.

Deus, ✠ qui humánæ substántiæ dignitátem mirabíliter condidísti, et mirabílius reformásti: da nobis per húius aquæ et vini mystérium, eius divinitátis esse consórtes, qui humanitátis nostræ fíeri dignátus est párticeps, Jesus Christus Fílius tuus Dóminus noster: Qui tecum vivit et regnat in unitáte Spíritus Sancti Deus: per ómnia sæcula sæculórum. Amen.

Then the priest takes the chalice, and offers it, saying:

Offérimus tibi, Dómine, cálicem salutáris, tuam deprecántes cleméntiam: ut in conspéctu divínæ majestátis tuæ, pro nostra et totíus mundi salúte, cum odóre suavitátis ascéndat. Amen.

The priest makes the Sign of the Cross with the chalice, places it upon the corporal, and covers it with the pall. Then, with his hands joined upon the Altar, and bowing down, he says:

ACCEPT, O Holy Father, Almighty and Eternal God, this spotless host, which I, Your unworthy servant, offer to You, my living and true God, to atone for my numberless sins, offenses, and negligences; on behalf of all here present and likewise for all faithful Christians living and dead, that it may avail me and them as a means of salvation to life everlasting. Amen.

Offering of the Chalice

Making the Sign of the Cross with the paten, the Priest places the host upon the corporal. He pours wine and water into the chalice, blessing the water before it is mixed, in remembrance of the water and blood which flowed from the side of Jesus.

O God, ✠ Who in creating man exalted his nature very wonderfully, and yet more wonderfully established it anew; by the Mystery signified in the mingling of this water and wine, grant us to have part in the Godhead of Him Who has deigned to become a partaker of our humanity, Jesus Christ, Thy Son our Lord; Who lives and reigns with Thee, in the unity of the Holy Spirit, God, world without end. Amen.

Then the Priest takes the chalice, and offers it, saying:

We offer unto Thee, O Lord, the chalice of salvation, entreating Thy mercy that our offering may ascend with a sweet fragrance in the sight of Thy divine Majesty, for our own salvation, and for that of the whole world. Amen.

The Priest makes the Sign of the Cross with the chalice, places it upon the corporal, and covers it. Bowing down, he says:

In spíritu humilitátis et in ánimo contríto suscipiámur a te, Dómine: et sic fiat sacrifícium nostrum in conspéctu tuo hódie, ut pláceat tibi, Dómine Deus.

Veni, Sanctificátor, omnípotens ætérne Deus: et benedicit oblata prosequendo: et béne ✠ dic hoc sacrifícium, tuo sancto nómini præparátum.

THE WASHING OF THE HANDS

The Priest washes his fingers, symbolizing the great purity and inner cleanliness necessary to offer or participate in this great Sacrifice.

LÁVABO inter innocéntes manus meas: et circúmdabo altáre tuum, Dómine.
Ut áudiam vocem laudis: et enárrem univérsa mirabília tua.
Dómine, diléxi decórem domus tuæ: et locum habitatiónis glóriæ tuæ.
Ne perdas cum ímpiis, Deus, ánimam meam: et cum viris sánguinum vitam meam.
In quorum mánibus iniquitátes sunt: déxtera eórum repléta est munéribus.
Ego autem in innocéntia mea ingréssus sum: rédime me, et miserére mei.
Pes meus stetit in diré cto: in ecclésiis benedícam te, Dómine.

Glória Patri, et Fílio, et Spirítui Sancto.
Sicut erat in princípio, et nunc, et semper: et in sæcula sæculórum. Amen.

Humbled in spirit and contrite of heart, may we find favor with Thee, O Lord: and may our sacrifice be so offered this day in Thy sight as to be pleasing to Thee, O Lord God.

Come Thou, the Sanctifier, Almighty and Everlasting God, and bless ✠ this sacrifice which is prepared for the glory of Thy holy Name.

THE WASHING OF THE HANDS

The Priest washes his fingers to participate in this great Sacrifice.

I will wash my hands among the innocent, and I will encompass Thy Altar, O Lord.
That I may hear the voice of praise, and tell of all Thy wondrous works.
I have loved, O Lord, the beauty of Thy house, and the place where Thy glory dwells.
Take not away my soul, O God, with the wicked, nor my life with men of blood.

In whose hands are iniquities: their right hand is filled with gifts.
But as for me, I have walked in my innocence; redeem me, and have mercy on me.
My foot has stood in the right way; in the churches I will bless Thee, O Lord.

Glory be to the Father, and to the Son, and to the Holy Spirit.
As it was in the beginning, is now, and ever shall be, world without end. Amen.

The Priest bows before the middle of Altar, and says:

Súscipe, sancta Trínitas, hanc oblatiónem, quam tibi offérimus ob memóriam Passiónis, Resurrectiónis, et Ascensiónis Jesu Christi, Dómini nostri, et in honórem beátæ Maríæ semper Vírginis, et beáti Joánnis Baptístæ, et sanctórum Apostolórum Petri et Páuli, et istórum, et ómnium sanctórum: ut illis profíciat ad honórem, nobis autem ad salútem: et illi pro nobis intercédere dignéntur in cælis, quorum memóriam ágimus in terris. Per eúndem Christum Dóminum nostrum. Amen.

Then, joining his hands and bowing before the tabernacle, the Priest turns to the people, extends and rejoins his hands and says:

P. Oráte fratres, ut meum ac vestrum sacrifícium acceptábile fiat apud Deum Patrem omnipoténtem.

S. *Suscípiat Dóminus sacrifícium de mánibus tuis ad láudem et glóriam nóminis sui, ad utilitátem quoque nostram, totiúsque Ecclésiæ suæ sanctæ.*

P. Amen.

THE SECRET

(Turn to appropriate Missal page)

Extending his hands, the Priest prays the Secret prayer.

P. Per ómnia sæcula sæculórum.

S. *Amen.*

The Priest bows before the middle of Altar, and says:

Receive, O Holy Trinity, this oblation which we make to Thee in memory of the Passion, Resurrection, and Ascension of our Lord Jesus Christ; and in honor of Blessed Mary ever Virgin, of blessed John the Baptist, of the holy Apostles Peter and Paul, of these *(relics of the Saints on the Altar),* and of all the Saints. To them let it bring honor, and to us salvation, and may they whom we are commemorating here on earth deign to plead for us in heaven. Through the same Christ our Lord. Amen.

Then, joining his hands and bowing before the tabernacle, the Priest turns to the people, extends and rejoins his hands and says:

P. Pray, brethren, that my sacrifice and yours may be acceptable to God the Father almighty.

S. May the Lord receive the sacrifice at your hands, for the praise and glory of His name, for our good, and the good of all His holy Church.

P. Amen.

THE SECRET

(Turn to appropriate Missal page)

Extending his hands, the Priest prays the Secret prayer.

P. World without end.

S. Amen.

PREFACE—CANON

P. Dóminus vobíscum.

S. *Et cum spíritu tuo.*

P. Sursum corda.

S. *Habémus ad Dóminum.*

P. Grátias agámus Dómino Deo nostro.

S. *Dignum et justum est.*

Preface for Sundays (the Most Holy Trinity)

Vere dignum et justum est, æquum et salutáre, nos tibi semper, et ubíque grátias ágere: Dómine sancte, Pater omnípotens, ætérne Deus: Qui cum unigénito Fílio tuo, et Spíritu Sancto, unus es Deus, unus es Dóminus: non in unívs singularitáte persónæ, sed in unívs Trinitáte substántiæ. Quod enim de tua glória, reveláte te, crédimus, hoc de Fílio tuo, hoc de Spíritu Sancto, sine differéntia discretiónis sentímus. Ut in confessióne veræ sempiternæque Deitátis, et in persónis propríetas, et in esséntia ùnitas, et in majestáte adorétur æquálitas. Quam laudant Angeli atque Archángeli, Chérubim quoque ac Séraphim: qui non cessant clamáre quotídie, una voce dicéntes:

The bells are rung three times.

KNEEL

PREFACE—CANON

P. The Lord be with you.
S. And with thy spirit.
P. Lift up your hearts.
S. We have lifted them up to the Lord.
P. Let us give thanks to the Lord our God.
S. It is right and just.

Preface for Sundays (the Most Holy Trinity)

It is truly fitting and just, right for our salvation, that we should at all times and in all places, give thanks unto Thee, O holy Lord, Father Almighty, Everlasting God; Who, together with Thy only-begotten Son, and the Holy Spirit, art one God, one Lord: not in the oneness of a single Person, but in the Trinity of one substance. For what we believe by Thy revelation of Thy glory, the same do we believe of Thy Son, the same of the Holy Spirit, without difference or separation. So that, in confessing the true and everlasting Godhead, distinction in persons, unity in essence, and equality in majesty may be adored. Which the Angels and Archangels, the Cherubim also and the Seraphim do praise: who cease not daily to cry out, with one voice saying:

KNEEL

The Sanctus

SANCTUS, Sanctus, Sanctus, Dóminus Deus Sábaoth. Pleni sunt cæli et terra glória tua. Hosánna in excélsis. ✠ Benedíctus qui venit in nómine Dómini. Hosánna in excélsis.

The Preface for Weekdays

The following Preface is said throughout the year on all weekdays and feasts with no proper Preface.

Vere dignum et justum est, æquum et salutáre, nos tibi semper, et ubíque grátias ágere: Dómine sancte, Pater omnípotens, ætérne Deus: per Christum Dóminum nostrum. Per quem majestátem tuam laudant Ángeli, adórant Dominatiónes, tremunt Potestátes. Coeli, coelorúmque Virtútes, ac beáta Séraphim, sócia exsultatióne concélebrant. Cum quibus et nostras voces, ut admítti júbeas deprecámur, súpplici confessióne dicéntes:

SANCTUS, Sanctus, Sanctus, Dóminus Deus Sábaoth. Pleni sunt cæli et terra glória tua. Hosánna in excélsis. ✠ Benedíctus qui venit in nómine Dómini. Hosánna in excélsis.

The Sanctus

HOLY, holy, holy, Lord God of Hosts. Heaven and earth are full of Thy Glory. Hosanna in the highest. ✠ Blessed is He Who comes in the Name of the Lord. Hosanna in the highest.

The Preface for Weekdays

The following Preface is said throughout the year on all weekdays and feasts with no proper Preface.

It is truly fitting and just, right for our salvation, that we should at all times and in all places, give thanks unto Thee, O holy Lord, Father almighty, everlasting God; through Christ Our Lord. Through Him the angels praise, the dominations adore, the powers, trembling with awe, worship Thy majesty: which the heavens and the forces of heaven, together with the blessed Seraphim, joyfully do magnify. And do Thou command that it be permitted to our lowliness to join with them in confessing Thee and unceasingly to repeat:

HOLY, holy, holy, Lord God of Hosts. Heaven and earth are full of Thy Glory. Hosanna in the highest. ✠ Blessed is He Who comes in the Name of the Lord. Hosanna in the highest.

THE CANON OF THE MASS

The Priest prays silently first for the Church.

Te igitur, clementíssime Pater, per Jesum Christum, Fílium tuum, Dóminum nostrum, súpplices rogámus ac pétimus, *(the Priest kisses the Altar)* uti accépta hábeas, et benedícas haec ✠ dona, haec ✠ múnera, hæc ✠ sancta sacrifícia illibáta; in primis, quæ tibi offérimus pro Ecclésia tua sancta cathólica; quam pacificáre, custodíre, adunáre, et régere dignéris toto orbe terrárum: una cum fámulo tuo Papa nostro *N.*, et Antístite nostro *N.*, et ómnibus orthodóxis, atque cathólicæ et apostólicæ fídei cultóribus.

THE CANON OF THE MASS

The Priest prays silently first for the Church.

Most merciful Father, we humbly pray and beseech Thee, through Jesus Christ Thy Son, Our Lord, *(The Priest kisses the Altar)* to accept and to bless these ✠ gifts, these ✠ presents, these ✠ holy unspotted Sacrifices, which we offer up to Thee, in the first place, for Thy Holy Catholic Church, that it may please Thee to grant her peace, to preserve, unite, and govern her throughout the world; as also for Thy servant *N.*, our Pope, and *N.*, our Bishop, and for all orthodox believers and all who profess the Catholic and Apostolic faith.

COMMEMORATION OF THE LIVING

Meménto, Dómine, famulórum famularúmque tuarum *N* . et N., *(the Priest prays for all the living he wishes to remember)* et ómnium circumstántium, quorum tibi fides cógnita est, et nota devótio, pro quibus tibi offérimus: vel qui tibi ófferunt hoc sacrifícium laudis, pro se, suísque ómnibus: pro redemptióne animárum suárum, pro spe salútis et incolumitátis suæ: tibíque reddunt vota sua ætérno Deo, vivo et vero.

COMMEMORATION OF THE SAINTS

Communicántes, et memóriam venerántes, in primis gloriósæ semper Vírginis Maríæ, Genitrícis Dei et Dómini nostri Jesu Christi: sed et beáti Joseph, eiúsdem Vírginis Sponsi, et beatórum Apostolórum ac Mártyrum tuórum, Petri et Páuli, Andréæ, Jacóbi, Joánnis, Thómæ, Jacóbi, Philíppi, Bartholomæi, Matthæi, Simónis, et Thaddæi: Lini, Cleti, Cleméntis, Xysti, Cornélii, Cypriáni, Lauréntii, Chrysógoni, Joánnis et Páuli, Cosmæ et Damiáni: et ómnium Sanctórum tuórum; quorum méritis precibúsque concédas, ut in ómnibus protectiónis tuæ muniámur auxilio. Per eúndem Christum Dóminum nostrum. Amen.

The Priest extends his hands over the oblation.
Here the bell is rung once.

COMMEMORATION OF THE LIVING

Be mindful, O Lord, of Thy servants and handmaids *N.* et *N.*, *(The Priest prays for all the living he wishes to remember before the Lord)* and of all here present, whose faith and devotion are known to Thee, for whom we offer, or who offer up to Thee this Sacrifice of praise for themselves and all those dear to them, for the redemption of their souls and the hope of their safety and salvation: who now pay their vows to Thee, the everlasting, living and true God.

COMMEMORATION OF THE SAINTS

In communion with, and honoring the memory in the first place of the glorious ever Virgin Mary Mother of our God and Lord Jesus Christ: also of blessed Joseph, her Spouse; and likewise of Thy blessed Apostles and Martyrs, Peter and Paul, Andrew, James, John, Thomas, James, Philip, Bartholomew, Matthew, Simon and Thaddeus, Linus, Cletus, Clement, Sixtus, Cornelius, Cyprian, Lawrence, Chrysogonus, John and Paul, Cosmas and Damian, and of all Thy Saints, grant for the sake of their merits and prayers that in all things we may be guarded and helped by Thy protection. Through the same Christ our Lord. Amen.

The Priest extends his hands over the oblation.

HANC ígitur oblatiónem servitútis nostræ, sed et cunctæ famíliæ tuæ, quæsumus, Dómine, ut placátus accípias: diésque nostros in tua pace dispónas, atque ab ætérna damnatióne nos éripi, et in electórum tuórum júbeas grege numerári. Per Christum Dóminum nostrum. Amen.

Quam oblatiónem tu, Deus, in ómnibus, quæsumus, bene✠ díctam, adscríp ✠ tam, ra ✠ tam, rationábilem, acceptabilémque fácere dignéris: ut nobis Cor ✠ pus, et Sán ✠ guis fiat dilectíssimi Fílii tui, Dómini nostri Jesu Christi.

THE CONSECRATION OF THE HOST

The Priest takes the host in his hands and says:

Qui prídie quam paterétur, accépit panem in sanctus ac venerábiles manus suas, et elevátis óculis in cælum ad te Deum, Patrem suum omnipoténtem, tibi grátias agens, bene díxit, fregit, dedítque discípulis suis, dicens: Accípite, et manducáte ex hoc omnes:

The Priest bows low and says:

HOC EST ENIM CORPUS MEUM.

O LORD, we beseech Thee, graciously to accept this oblation of our service and that of Thy whole household. Order our days in Thy peace, and command that we be rescued from eternal damnation and numbered in the flock of Thy elect. Through Christ our Lord. Amen.

Humbly we pray Thee, O God, be pleased to make this same offering wholly blessed ✠, to consecrate ✠ it and approve ✠ it, making it reasonable and acceptable, so that it may become for us the Body ✠ and Blood ✠ of Thy dearly beloved Son, our Lord Jesus Christ.

THE CONSECRATION OF THE HOST

The Priest takes the host in his hands and says:

Who, the day before He suffered, took bread into His holy and venerable hands, and having lifted up His eyes to heaven, to Thee, God, His Almighty Father, giving thanks to Thee, blessed it , broke it, and gave it to His disciples, saying: Take and eat ye all of this:

The Priest bows low and says:

FOR THIS IS MY BODY.

As the Priest adores and elevates the Sacred Host.
gaze on it and say devoutly, "My Lord and My God!"
The bell is rung three times.

THE CONSECRATION OF THE WINE

The Priest uncovers the chalice and says,

Símili modo póstquam coenátum est, accípiens et hunc præclárum Cálicem in sanctas ac venerábiles manus suas: item tibi grátias agens, bene ✠ díxit, dedítque discípulis suis, dicens: Accípite, et bíbite ex eo omnes:

As the Priest adores and elevates the Sacred Host.
gaze on it and say devoutly, "My Lord and My God!"

THE CONSECRATION OF THE WINE

The Priest uncovers the chalice and says,

In like manner, after He had supped, taking also into His holy and venerable hands this goodly chalice, again giving thanks to Thee, He blessed it, ✠ and gave it to His disciples, saying: Take and drink ye all of this:

The Priest bends over the chalice
and pronounces these words:

HIC EST ENIM CALIX SÁNGUINIS MEI,
NOVI ET ÆTÉRNI TESTAMÉNTI:
MYSTÉRIUM FIDEI:
QUI PRO VOBIS ET PRO MULTIS
EFFUNDÉTUR
IN REMISSIÓNEM PECCATÓRUM.

Hæc quotiescúmque fecéritis, in mei memóriam faciétis.

The Priest adores the Precious Blood of Jesus as he elevates the chalice.
The bell is rung three times.

The Priest bends over the chalice and pronounces these words:

FOR THIS IS THE CHALICE OF MY BLOOD, OF THE NEW AND ETERNAL TESTAMENT: THE MYSTERY OF FAITH: WHICH WILL BE SHED FOR YOU AND FOR MANY UNTO THE REMISSION OF SINS.

As often as ye shall do these things, ye shall do them in remembrance of me.

The Priest adores the Precious Blood of Jesus as he elevates the chalice. The bell is rung three times.

We offer Christ, the Pure Victim, to His Father

Unde et mémores, Dómine, nos servi tui, sed et plebs tua sancta, ejúsdem Christi Fílii tui, Dómini nostri, tam beátæ passiónis, nec non et ab ínferis resurrectiónis, sed et in cælos gloriósæ ascensiónis: offérimus præcláræ majestáti tuæ de tuis donis ac datis, hóstiam ✠ puram, hóstiam ✠ sanctam, hóstiam ✠ immaculátam, Panem ✠ sanctum vitæ ætérnæ, et Cálicem ✠ salútis perpétuæ.

Supra quæ propítio ac seréno vultu respícere dignéris: et accépta habére, sícuti accépta habére dignátus es múnera púeri tui justi Abel, et sacrifícium Patriárchæ nostri Abrahæ: et quod tibi óbtulit summus sacérdos tuus Melchísedech, sanctum sacrifícium, immaculátam hóstiam.

Bowing down, the Priest prays:

Súpplices te rogámus, omnípotens Deus, jube hæc perférri per manus sancti Angeli tui in sublíme altáre tuum, in conspéctu divínæ majestátis tuæ: ut quotquot *(the Priest kisses the Altar)* ex hac altáris participatióne sacrosánctum Fílii tui Cor ✠ pus et Sán ✠ guinem sumpsérimus, omni benedictióne cælésti et grátia repleámur. Per eúndem Christum Dóminum nostrum. Amen.

We offer Christ, the Pure Victim, to His Father

And now, O Lord, we, Thy servants, and with us all Thy holy people, calling to mind the blessed Passion of this same Christ, Thy Son, our Lord, likewise His Resurrection from the grave, and also His glorious Ascension into heaven, do offer unto Thy most sovereign Majesty out of the gifts Thou hast bestowed upon us, a Victim ✠ which is pure, a Victim ✠ which is holy, a Victim ✠ which is spotless, the holy Bread ✠ of life eternal, and the Chalice ✠ of everlasting Salvation.

Deign to look upon them with a favorable and gracious countenance, and to accept them as Thou did accept the offerings of Thy just servant Abel, and the sacrifice of our Patriarch Abraham, and that which Thy high priest Melchisedech offered up to Thee, a holy Sacrifice, an immaculate Victim.

Bowing down, the Priest prays:

We most humbly beseech Thee, almighty God, command these offerings to be borne by the hands of Thy holy Angel to Thy Altar on high, in the sight of Thy divine majesty, that as many *(the Priest kisses the Altar)* as shall partake of the most holy Body ✠ and Blood ✠ of Thy Son at this Altar, may be filled with every heavenly grace and blessing. Through the same Christ our Lord. Amen.

COMMEMORATION OF THE DEAD

We pray for our dearly departed loved ones and benefactors.

Meménto étiam, Dómine, famulórum famularúmque tuárum N. et N., qui nos præcessérunt cum signo fídei, et dórmiunt in somno pacis.

The Priest prays for the dead he wishes to remember; then extending his hands he proceeds:

Ipsis, Dómine, et ómnnibus in Christo quiescéntibus, locum refrigérii, lucis et pacis, ut indúlgeas, deprecámur. Per eúndem Christum Dóminum nostrum. Amen.

The Priest pronounces the next few words in a somewhat elevated tone of voice; at the same time he strikes his breast in a token of contrition.

Nobis quoque peccatóribus fámulis tuis, de multitúdine miseratiónum tuárum sperántibus, partem áliquam, et societátem donáre dignéris, cum tuis sanctis Apóstolis et Martýribus: cum Joánne, Stéphano, Matthía, Bárnaba, Ignátio, Alexándro, Marcellíno, Petro, Felicitáte, Perpétua, Agatha, Lúcia, Agnéte, Cæcília, Anastásia, et ómnibus Sanctis tuis: intra quorum nos consórtium, non æstimátor mériti, sed véniæ, quæsumus, largítor admítte. Per Christum Dóminum nostrum.

COMMEMORATION OF THE DEAD

Mention your departed parents, grandparents, relatives, friends, benefactors, and teachers.

Remember also, O Lord, Thy servants and handmaids *N.* and *N.*, who are gone before us with the sign of faith, and rest in the sleep of peace.

The Priest prays for the dead he wishes to remember; then extending his hands he proceeds:

To these, O Lord, and to all that rest in Christ, grant, we beseech Thee, a place of refreshment, light, and peace. Through the same Christ our Lord. Amen.

The Priest pronounces the next few words in a somewhat elevated tone of voice; at the same time he strikes his breast in a token of contrition.

To us also Thy sinful servants, who put our trust in the multitude of Thy mercies, deign to grant some part and fellowship with Thy holy Apostles and Martyrs: with John, Stephen, Matthias, Barnabas, Ignatius, Alexander, Marcellinus, Peter, Felicitas, Perpetua, Agatha, Lucy, Agnes, Cecilia, Anastasia, and all Thy Saints. Into their company we beseech Thee admit us, not considering our merits, but freely pardoning our offenses. Through Christ our Lord.

Per quem hæc ómnia, Dómine, semper bona creas, sanctí✠ficas, viví✠ficas, bene✠dícis, et præstas nobis.

The Priest uncovers the Chalice, and genuflects: then taking the Host and Chalice, he makes the Sign of the Cross five times over the Chalice, saying:

THE MINOR ELEVATION

Per ip✠sum, et cum ip✠so, et in ip✠so, est tibi Deo Patri ✠ omnipoténti, in unitáte Spíritus✠Sancti, omnis honor et glória.

The Priest elevates the Host and Chalice. Replacing the Host, and covering the Chalice, he genuflects, rises, and says:

P. Per ómnia sæcula sæculórum.

S. *Amen.*

COMMUNION

THE PATER NOSTER

The Priest sings or says aloud the Lord's Prayer.

Orémus. Præcéptis salutáribus móniti, et divína institutióne formáti, audémus dícere:

By Whom, O Lord, Thou do ever create, sanctify, ✠ quicken, ✠ bless, ✠ and give unto us all these good things.

The Priest uncovers the Chalice, and genuflects: then taking the Host and Chalice, he makes the Sign of the Cross five times over the Chalice, saying:

THE MINOR ELEVATION

Through Him, ✠ and with Him, ✠ and in Him, ✠ is unto Thee, God the Father ✠ almighty, in the unity of the Holy ✠ Spirit, all honor and glory.

The Priest elevates the Host and Chalice. Replacing the Host, and covering the Chalice, he kneels down, rises, and says:

P. World without end.

S. Amen.

COMMUNION

THE PATER NOSTER

The Priest sings or says aloud the Lord's Prayer, taught us by the Savior Himself.

P. Let us pray. Admonished by Thy saving precepts and following Thy divine instruction, we make bold to say:

PATER NOSTER, qui es in cælis: Sanctificétur nomen tuum: Advéniat regnum tuum: Fiat volúntas tua, sicut in cælo, et in terra. Panem nostrum quotidiánum da nobis hódie: Et dimítte nobis débita nostra, sicut et nos dimíttimus debitóribus nostris. Et ne nos indúcas in tentatiónem:

S. *Sed líbera nos a malo.*

P. Amen.

Líbera nos, quæsumus, Dómine, ab ómnibus malis, prætéritis, præséntibus, et futúris: et intercedénte beáta et gloriósa semper Vírgine Dei Genitríce María, cum beátis Apóstolis tuis Petro et Paulo, atque Andréa, et ómnibus Sanctis, ✠ da propítius pacem in diébus nostris: ut ope misericórdiæ tuæ adjúti, et a peccáto simus semper líberi, et ab omni perturbatióne secúri.

The Priest uncovers the chalice, genuflects, takes the Host, and breaking it down the middle over the chalice says:

Per eúndem Dóminum nostrum Jesum Christum Fílium tuum. Qui tecum vivit et regnat in unitáte Spíritus Sancti Deus.

P. Per ómnia sæcula sæculórum.

S. *Amen.*

P. Pax ✠ Dómini sit ✠ semper vobís ✠ cum.

S. *Et cum spíritu tuo.*

OUR FATHER, Who art in heaven, hallowed be Thy Name. Thy kingdom come; Thy will be done on earth as it is in heaven. Give us this day our daily bread; and forgive us our trespasses, as we forgive those who trespass against us. And lead us not into temptation.

S. But deliver us from evil.

P. Amen.

Deliver us, we beseech Thee, O Lord, from all evils, past, present, and to come, and by the intercession of the Blessed and glorious ever Virgin Mary, Mother of God, together with Thy blessed apostles Peter and Paul, and Andrew, and all the Saints, ✠ mercifully grant peace in our days, that through the bounteous help of Thy mercy we may be always free from sin, and safe from all disquiet.

The Priest uncovers the chalice, genuflects, takes the Host, and breaking it down the middle over the chalice says:

Through the same Jesus Christ, Thy Son our Lord, Who lives and reigns with Thee in the unity of the Holy Spirit, God,

P. World without end.

S. Amen.

P. May the peace ✠ of the Lord be ✠ always ✠ with you.

S. And with thy spirit.

The Priest places the Particle in the chalice and says quietly:

Hæc commíxtio et consecrátio Córporis et Sánguinis Dómini nostri Jesu Christi, fiat accipiéntibus nobis in vitam ætérnam. Amen.

Bowing down the Priest prays:

AGNUS DEI, qui tollis peccáta mundi: miserére nobis.

Agnus Dei, qui tollis peccáta mundi: miserére nobis.

Agnus Dei, qui tollis peccáta mundi: dona nobis pacem.

PRAYERS BEFORE HOLY COMMUNION

In Requiem Masses, the following prayer is omitted.

Dómine Jesu Christe, qui dixísti Apóstolis tuis: Pacem relínquo vobis, pacem meam do vobis: ne respícias peccáta mea, sed fidem Ecclésiæ tuæ; eámque secúndum voluntátem tuam pacificáre et coadunáre dignéris: Qui vivis et regnas Deus per ómnia sæcula sæculórum. Amen.

The Priest places the Particle in the chalice and says quietly:

May this mingling and hallowing of the Body and Blood of our Lord Jesus Christ be for us who receive it a source of eternal life. Amen.

Bowing down the Priest prays:

LAMB OF GOD, Who takes away the sins of the world, have mercy on us.

Lamb of God, Who takes away the sins of the world, have mercy on us.

Lamb of God, Who takes away the sins of the world, grant us peace.

PRAYERS BEFORE HOLY COMMUNION

In Requiem Masses, the following prayer is omitted.

O Lord, Jesus Christ, Who did say to Thy Apostles: Peace I leave you, My peace I give to you: look not upon my sins, but upon the faith of Thy Church; and deign to give her that peace and unity which is agreeable to Thy will: God Who lives and reigns world without end. Amen.

Prayer for Holiness

Dómine Jesu Christe, Fili Dei vivi, qui ex voluntáte Patris, cooperánte Spíritu Sancto, per mortem tuam mundum vivificásti: líbera me per hoc sacrosánctum Corpus et Sánguinem tuum ab ómnibus iniquitátibus meis et univérsis malis: et fac me tuis semper inhærére mandátis, et a te numquam separári permíttas: Qui cum eódem Deo Patre, et Spiritu Sancto vivis et regnas Deus in sæcula sæculórum. Amen.

Prayer for Grace

Percéptio Córporis tui, Dómine Jesu Christe, quod ego indígnus súmere præsúmo, non mihi provéniat in judícium et condemnatiónem: sed pro tua pietáte prosit mihi ad tutaméntum mentis et córporis, et ad medélam percipiéndam: Qui vivis et regnas cum Deo Patre in unitáte Spíritus Sancti Deus, per ómnia sæcula sæculórum. Amen.

COMMUNION OF THE PRIEST

Panem cæléstem accípiam, et nomen Dómini invocábo.

Striking his breast, the Priest says the following three times with the first words audible; The bells are rung three times.

Dómine, non sum dignus, ut intres sub tectum meum: sed tantum dic verbo, et sanábitur ánima mea.

Prayer for Holiness

O Lord Jesus Christ, Son of the living God, Who, by the will of the Father and the co-operation of the Holy Spirit, has by Thy death given life to the world: deliver me by this, Thy most sacred Body and Blood, from all my iniquities and from every evil; make me cling always to Thy commandments, and permit me never to be separated from Thee. Who with the same God, the Father and the Holy Spirit, lives and reigns God, world without end. Amen.

Prayer for Grace

Let not the partaking of Thy Body, O Lord Jesus Christ, which I, though unworthy, presume to receive, turn to my judgment and condemnation; but through Thy mercy may it be unto me a safeguard and a healing remedy both of soul and body. Who lives and reigns with God the Father, in the unity of the Holy Spirit, God, world without end. Amen.

COMMUNION OF THE PRIEST

I will take the Bread of Heaven, and will call upon the name of the Lord.

Striking his breast he says the following three times with the first words audible:

Lord, I am not worthy that Thou shouldst enter under my roof; but only say the word, and my soul shall be healed.

The Priest makes the Sign of the Cross with the Host over the paten, saying silently:

Corpus Dómini nostri Jesu Christi custódiat ánimam meam in vitam ætérnam. Amen.

He consumes the Host, uncovers the chalice, genuflects and continues silently:

Quid retríbuam Dómino pro ómnibus quæ retríbuit mihi? Cálicem salutáris accípiam, et nomen Dómini invocábo. Láudans invocábo Dóminum, et ab inimícis meis salvus ero.

He makes the Sign of the Cross with the chalice and says:

Sanguis Dómini nostri Jesu Christi custódiat ánimam meam in vitam ætérnam. Amen.

The Priest drinks the Precious Blood.

COMMUNION OF THE FAITHFUL

The server prays the Confiteor. The Priest turns to the people and says:

P. Misereátur vestri omnípotens Deus, et dimíssis peccátis vestris, perdúcat vos ad vitam æternam.

S. *Amen.*

The Priest makes the Sign of the Cross with the Host over the paten, saying silently:

May the Body of Our Lord Jesus Christ preserve my soul unto life everlasting. Amen.

He consumes the Host, uncovers the chalice, genuflects and continues silently:

What return shall I make to the Lord for all the things that He has given unto me? I will take the chalice of salvation, and call upon the Name of the Lord. I will call upon the Lord and give praise: and I shall be saved from mine enemies.

He makes the Sign of the Cross with the chalice and says:

May the Blood of Our Lord Jesus Christ preserve my soul unto life everlasting. Amen.

He drinks the Precious Blood.

COMMUNION OF THE FAITHFUL

The server prays the Confiteor. The Priest turns to the people and says:

P. May Almighty God have mercy upon you, forgive you your sins, and bring you to life everlasting.

S. Amen.

P. Indulgéntiam, ✠ absolutiónem, et remissiónem peccatórum vestrórum, tríbuat vobis omnípotens et miséricors Dóminus.

S. *Amen.*

The Priest genuflects, elevates the Host and turning towards the people says:

Ecce Agnus Dei, ecce qui tollit peccáta mundi.

Dómine, non sum dignus, ut intres sub tectum meum: sed tantum dic verbo, et sanábitur ánima mea. *(Three times)*

The Priest distributes Communion to the faithful, saying to each person:

Corpus Dómini nostri Jesu Christi custódiat ánimam tuam in vitam æternam. Amen.

P. May the Almighty and merciful Lord grant you pardon, ✠ absolution, and remission of your sins.

S. Amen.

The Priest genuflects, elevates the Host before the people and says:

Behold the Lamb of God, behold Him Who takes away the sins of the world.

Lord, I am not worthy that Thou shouldst enter under my roof; but only say the word, and my soul shall be healed. *(Three times)*

The Priest distributes Communion to the faithful, saying to each:

May the Body of Our Lord Jesus Christ preserve your soul unto life everlasting. Amen.

THE ABLUTIONS

After Communion the Priest puts any extra Hosts into the tabernacle and taking the chalice, has the server pour in wine. He drinks it and says quietly:

Quod ore súmpsimus, Dómine, pura mente capiámus: et de múnere temporáli fiat nobis remédium sempitérnum.

Wine and water are poured into the chalice over the Priest's fingers. As he dries them he says quietly:

Corpus tuum, Dómine, quod sumpsi, et Sanguis, quem potávi, adhæreat viscéribus meis: et præsta; ut in me non remáneat scélerum mácula, quem pura et sancta refecérunt sacraménta: Qui vivis et regnas in sæcula sæculorum. Amen.

He drinks the wine and water, cleans the chalice and veils it.

COMMUNION AND POSTCOMMUNION

(Turn to appropriate Missal page)

The Priest goes to the right side of the Altar and reads the Communion verse.

Moving to the middle of the Altar the Priest says:

P. Dóminus vobíscum.

S. *Et cum spíritu tuo.*

P. Orémus.

THE ABLUTIONS

After Communion the Priest puts any extra Hosts into the tabernacle and the server pours wine into the chalice. He drinks it, saying quietly:

Grant, O Lord, that what we have taken with our mouth, we may receive with a pure mind; and that from a temporal gift it may become for us an everlasting remedy.

Wine and water are poured into the chalice over the Priest's fingers. As he dries them he says quietly:

May Thy Body, O Lord, which I have received and Thy Blood which I have drunk, cleave to my inmost parts, and grant that no stain of sin remain in me; whom these pure and holy Sacraments have refreshed. Who lives and reigns world without end. Amen.

He drinks the wine and water, cleans the chalice and veils it.

COMMUNION AND POSTCOMMUNION

(Turn to appropriate Missal page)

The Priest reads the Communion verse.
Moving to the middle of the Altar the Priest says:

P. The Lord be with you.

S. And with thy spirit.

P. Let us pray.

The Priest returns to the right side of the Altar and reads the Postcommunion.

S. *Amen.*

FINAL PRAYERS

Returning to the middle of the Altar, the Priest kisses it and turns to the people, saying:

P. Dóminus vobíscum.

S. *Et cum spíritu tuo.*

P. Ite, Missa est.

S. *Deo grátias.*

Bowing before the Altar, the Priest prays silently:

Pláceat tibi, sancta Trínitas, obséquium servitútis meæ: et præsta; ut sacrifícium, quod óculis tuæ majestátis indígnus óbtuli, tibi sit acceptábile, mihíque, et ómnibus, pro quibus illud óbtuli, sit, te miseránte, propitiábile. Per Christum Dóminum nostrum. Amen.

He kisses the Altar, turns to the people and blessing them says:

The Priest returns to the right side of the Altar and reads the Postcommunion.

S. Amen.

FINAL PRAYERS

Returning to the middle of the Altar, the Priest kisses it and turns to the people, saying:

P. The Lord be with you.

S. And with thy spirit.

P. Go, the Mass is ended.

S. Thanks be to God.

Bowing before the Altar, the Priest prays silently:

May the tribute of my homage be pleasing to Thee, O most holy Trinity. Grant that the Sacrifice which I, unworthy as I am, have offered in the presence of Thy Majesty, may be acceptable to Thee. Through Thy mercy may it bring forgiveness to me and to all for whom I have offered it. Through Christ our Lord. Amen.

He kisses the Altar, turns to the people and blessing them says:

P. Benedícat vos omnípotens Deus, Pater, ✠ et Fílius, et Spíritus Sanctus.

S. *Amen.*

THE LAST GOSPEL

STAND

The Priest goes to the left side of the Altar and says:

P. Dóminus vobíscum.

S. *Et cum spíritu tuo.*

P. ✠ Inítium sancti Evangélii secúndum Joánnem.

S. *Glória tibi, Dómine.*

P. May Almighty God bless you: the Father, ✠ the Son, and the Holy Spirit.

S. Amen.

THE LAST GOSPEL

STAND

The Priest goes to the left side of the Altar and says:

P. The Lord be with you.

S. And with thy spirit.

P. ✠ The beginning of the holy Gospel according to Saint John.

S. Glory be to Thee, O Lord.

In princípio erat Verbum, et Verbum erat apud Deum, et Deus erat Verbum. Hoc erat in princípio apud Deum. Omnia per ipsum facta sunt: et sine ipso factum est nihil, quod factum est: in ipso vita erat, et vita erat lux hóminum: et lux in ténebris lucet, et ténebræ eam non comprehendérunt.

Fuit homo missus a Deo, cui nomen erat Joánnes. Hic venit in testimónium, ut testimónium perhibéret de lúmine, ut omnes créderent per illum. Non erat ille lux, sed ut testimónium perhibéret de lúmine. Erat lux vera, quæ illúminat omnem hóminem veniéntem in hunc mundum.

In mundo erat, et mundus per ipsum factus est, et mundus eum non cognóvit. In própria venit, et sui eum non recepérunt. Quotquot autem recepérunt eum, dedit eis potestátem fílios Dei fíeri, his, qui credunt in nómine ejus: qui non ex sanguínibus, neque ex voluntáte carnis, neque ex voluntáte viri, sed ex Deo nati sunt.

(Genuflect) ET VERBUM CARO FACTUM EST, et habitávit in nobis: et vídimus glóriam ejus, glóriam quasi Unigéniti a Patre, plenum grátiæ et veritátis.

S. *Deo grátias.*

In the beginning was the Word, and the Word was with God, and the Word was God. The same was in the beginning with God. All things were made by Him, and without Him was made nothing that was made. In Him was life, and the life was the Light of men: and the Light shines in darkness, and the darkness did not comprehend it.

There was a man sent from God, whose name was John. This man came for a witness, to bear witness of the Light, that all men might believe through Him. He was not the Light, but was to bear witness of the Light.

That was the true Light, which enlightens every man that comes into this world. He was in the world, and the world was made by Him, and the world knew Him not. He came unto His own, and His own received Him not. But as many as received Him, to them He gave power to become the sons of God; to them that believe in His name: who are born, not of blood, nor of the will of the flesh, nor of the will of man, but of God.

(Genuflect) **AND THE WORD WAS MADE FLESH**, and dwelt among us, and we saw His glory, the glory as of the Only-begotten of the Father, full of grace and truth.

S. Thanks be to God.

PRAYERS AFTER LOW MASS

KNEEL

Hail Mary, full of grace, the Lord is with thee; blessed art thou among women, and blessed is the fruit of thy womb, Jesus. Holy Mary, Mother of God, pray for us sinners, now and at the hour of our death. Amen. *(Pray three times.)*

Hail, Holy Queen, Mother of Mercy, our life, our sweetness, and our hope. To thee do we cry, poor banished children of Eve. To thee do we send up our sighs, mourning and weeping in this valley of tears. Turn then, most gracious advocate, thine eyes of mercy towards us, and after this our exile, show unto us the blessed Fruit of thy womb, Jesus.

O clement, O loving, O sweet Virgin Mary.

P. Pray for us, O holy Mother of God.

S. That we may be made worthy of the promises of Christ.

P. **Let us pray.** O God, our refuge and our strength, look down with mercy upon Thy people who cry to Thee; and by the intercession of the glorious and Immaculate Virgin Mary, Mother of God, of Saint Joseph her spouse, of Thy blessed Apostles Peter and Paul, and of all the saints, mercifully and graciously hear the prayers which we pour forth for the conversion of sinners, and for the liberty and exaltation of our Holy Mother the Church. Through the same Christ Our Lord.

S. Amen.

Saint Michael the Archangel, defend us in battle; be our protection against the wickedness and snares of the devil. May God rebuke him, we humbly pray: and do thou, O Prince of the heavenly host, by the power of God, thrust into hell Satan and all the evil spirits who prowl about the world seeking the ruin of souls.

S. Amen.

P. Most Sacred Heart of Jesus,
S. Have mercy on us.

P. Most Sacred Heart of Jesus,
S. Have mercy on us.

P. Most Sacred Heart of Jesus,
S. Have mercy on us.

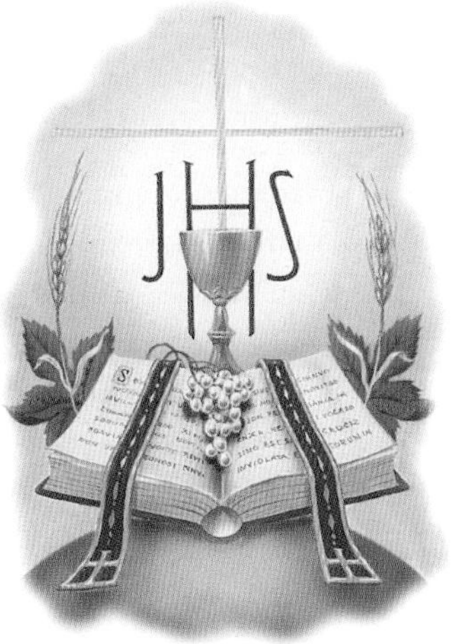

PRAYERS AFTER MASS

Prayer of Saint Ignatius of Loyola

Take O Lord, and receive all my liberty, my memory, my understanding, and my entire will. All that I am and all that I possess, You have given to me. I surrender it all to You; dispose of it according to Your will. Give me only Your love and Your grace; that's enough for me. With these I will be rich enough, and will desire nothing more. Amen.

Anima Christi

Soul of Christ, sanctify me;
Body of Christ, save me;
Blood of Christ, inebriate me;
Water from the side of Christ, wash me;
Passion of Christ, strengthen me;

O good Jesus, hear me;
Within Your wounds, hide me;
Separated from You, let me never be;
From the evil one, protect me;
At the hour of my death, call me;
And close to You, bid me;

That with Your saints, I may be,
Praising You forever and ever. Amen.

Prayer Before a Crucifix

Look down upon me, O good and gentle Jesus, while before Your face I humbly kneel, and with burning soul pray and beseech You to fix deep in my heart lively sentiments of faith, hope, and charity; true contrition for my sins, and a firm purpose of amendment, while I contemplate, with great love and tender pity, Your five most precious wounds, pondering over them within me and calling to mind the words which David, Your prophet, said of You, my Jesus: "They have pierced my hands and my feet; They have numbered all my bones." Amen.

According to the Enchiridion of Indulgences, revised in 1968, a ***plenary indulgence*** *is granted on each Friday of Lent and Passiontide to the faithful, who after Communion piously pray the above prayer before an image of Christ crucified; on other days of the year the indulgence is* ***partial.***

Prayer of Saint Thomas Aquinas

Lord, Father all-powerful and ever-living God, I thank You, for even though I am a sinner, Your unprofitable servant, not because of my worth but in the kindness of Your mercy, You have fed me with the Precious Body and Blood of Your Son, our Lord Jesus Christ.

I pray that this Holy Communion may not bring me condemnation and punishment, but forgiveness and salvation. May it be a helmet of faith and a shield of good will. May it purify me from evil ways and put an end to my evil passions. May it bring me charity and patience, humility and obedience, and growth in the power to do good.

May it be my strong defense against all my enemies, visible and invisible, and the perfect calming of all my evil impulses, bodily and spiritual. May it unite me more closely to you, the One true God, and lead me safely through death to everlasting happiness with You.

And I pray that You will lead me, a sinner, to the banquet where You, with Your Son and Holy Spirit, are true and perfect light, total fulfillment, everlasting joy, gladness without end, and perfect happiness to Your saints. Grant this through Christ our Lord. Amen.

Prayer of Saint Bonaventure

Saint Bonaventure, Franciscan, Bishop, and Doctor of the Church, was one of the most beloved men of God in the Middle Ages.

Pierce, O most Sweet Lord Jesus, my inmost soul with the most joyous and healthful wound of Thy love, with true, serene, and most holy apostolic charity, that my soul may ever languish and melt with love and longing for Thee, that it may yearn for Thee and faint for Thy courts, and long to be dissolved and to be with Thee.

Grant that my soul may hunger after Thee, the bread of angels, the refreshment of holy souls, our daily and super substantial bread, having all sweetness and savor and every delight of taste; let my heart ever hunger after and feed upon Thee, upon whom the angels desire to look, and may my inmost soul be filled with the sweetness of Thy savor; may it ever thirst after Thee, the fountain of life, the fountain of wisdom and knowledge, the fountain of eternal light, the torrent of pleasure, the richness of the house of God.

May it ever compass Thee, seek Thee, find Thee, run to Thee, attain Thee, meditate upon Thee, speak of Thee, and do all things to the praise and glory of Thy name, with humility and discretion, with love and delight, with ease and affection, and with perseverance unto the end; may Thou alone be ever my hope, my entire assurance, my riches, my delight, my pleasure, my joy, my rest and tranquility, my peace, my sweetness, my fragrance, my sweet savor, my food, my refreshment, my refuge, my help, my wisdom, my portion, my possession and my treasure, in whom may my mind and my heart be fixed and firmly rooted immovably henceforth and for ever. Amen.

DAILY MASS FOR THE DEAD

(NB: Prayers and Readings are taken from the 1962 Missal)

- *Beginning of the Mass, page 19.*

Introit: 4 Esdras 2:34-35. Eternal rest grant unto them, O Lord: and let perpetual light shine upon them. Psalm 64:2-3. A hymn, O God, awaits Thee in Sion, and a vow shall be paid to Thee in Jerusalem: O Lord, hear my prayer; all flesh shall come unto Thee. **V.** Eternal rest grant unto them, O Lord: and let perpetual light shine upon them.

- *Kyrie, page 27. Omit the Gloria.*

Prayer: O God, the Creator and Redeemer of all the faithful, grant to the souls of Thy servants and handmaids the remission of all their sins, that by devout prayers they may obtain the pardon which they ever desired. Who lives and reigns with God the Father, in the unity of the Holy Spirit, world without end. Amen.

Epistle: Apocalypse 14:13. In those days I heard a voice from Heaven, saying to me: "Write, blessed are the dead who die in the Lord. From henceforth now, saith the Spirit, that they may rest from their labors, for their works follow them."

Gradual: 4 Esdras 2:34-35. Eternal rest give to them, O Lord; and let perpetual light shine upon them. **V.** Psalm111:7. The just shall be in everlasting remembrance; he shall not fear the evil hearing.

Tract: Absolve, O Lord, the souls of all the faithful departed from every bond of sin. **V.** And by the help of Thy grace, let them be found worthy to escape the judgment of punishment. **V.** And to enjoy the happiness of light eternal.

Sequence—Dies Irae

Day of wrath, O day of mourning,
Lo, the world in ashes burning–
Seer and Sibyl gave the warning.

O what fear man's bosom rendeth,
When from Heaven the Judge descendeth,
On whose sentence all dependeth!

Wondrous sound the trumpet flingeth,
Through earth's sepulchres it ringeth,
All before the throne it bringeth.

Death is struck, and nature quaking,
All creation is awaking–
To its Judge an answer making.

Lo, the book, exactly worded,
Wherein all hath been recorded–
Thence shall judgment be awarded.

When the Judge His seat attaineth,
And each hidden deed arraigneth,
Nothing unavenged remaineth.

What shall I, frail man, be pleading?
Who for me be interceding,
When the just are mercy needing?

King, of majesty tremendous,
Who dost free salvation send us,
Fount of pity, then befriend us.

Think, kind Jesus, my salvation,
Caused Thy wondrous Incarnation–
Leave me not to reprobation.

Faint and weary, Thou hast sought me,
On the cross of suffering bought me;
Shall such grace be vainly brought me?

Righteous Judge of retribution,
Grant Thy gift of absolution
Ere that reck'ning day's conclusion.

Guilty, now I pour my moaning,
All my shame with anguish owning:
Spare, O God, Thy suppliant groaning.

Thou the sinful Mary savest,
Thou the dying thief forgavest,
And to me a hope vouchsafest.

Worthless are my prayers and sighing,
Yet, good Lord, in grace complying,
Rescue me from fires undying.

With Thy favored sheep, oh, place me;
Nor among the goats abase me,
But to Thy right hand upraise me.

While the wicked are confounded,
Doomed to flames of woe unbounded,
Call me, with Thy saints surrounded.

Low I kneel, with heart submission;
See, like ashes, my contrition–
Help me in my last condition.

Ah, that day of tears and mourning,
From the dust of earth returning,
Man for Judgment must prepare him–

Spare, O God, in mercy spare him.
Sweet Lord Jesus, who redeemed him,
Grant a blessed requiem. Amen.

- *Prayer: Cleanse My Heart, page 31.*

Gospel: John 6:51-55. At that time: Jesus said to the multitudes of the Jews: "I am the living bread which came down from heaven. If any man eat of this bread, he shall live for ever; and the bread that I will give is My Flesh, for the life of the world." The Jews therefore strove among themselves, saying: "How can this man give us His Flesh to eat?" Then Jesus said to them: "Amen, amen I say unto you: Except you eat the Flesh of the Son of Man, and drink His Blood, you shall not have life in you. He that eats My Flesh, and drinks My Blood, has everlasting life: and I will raise him up on the last day."

Offertory: O Lord Jesus Christ, King of glory, deliver the souls of all the faithful departed from the pains of Hell and from the deep pit: deliver them from the mouth of the lion, that Hell may not swallow them up, and they may not fall into darkness; but let Michael, the holy standard-bearer, bring them into the holy light which Thou did promise of old to Abraham and his seed. **V.** We offer Thee sacrifices and prayers of praise, O Lord; do Thou receive them for those souls whom we commemorate this day: grant them, O Lord, to pass from death to life, which of old Thou did promise to Abraham and to his seed.

• *Offertory Prayers, page 37.*

Secret: Mercifully look down, we beseech Thee, O Lord, upon the sacrifice which we offer Thee for the souls of Thy servants and handmaids, that, to those on whom Thou did confer the gift of Christian faith, Thou may also grant its reward. Through our Lord.

PREFACE FOR THE DEAD

It is truly fitting and proper, right and profitable to salvation, that we should at all times and in all places give thanks to Thee, O Lord, Holy Father, almighty and everlasting God, through Christ our Lord, in Whom has shone upon us the hope of a blessed resurrection, so that those who are afflicted by the certainty of dying, may be consoled by the promise of future immortality. For Thy Faithful, Lord, life is changed, not taken away; and when the abode of this earthly sojourn is destroyed, an eternal dwelling is prepared in Heaven. And therefore with Angels and Archangels, with the Thrones and Dominions, and with all the heavenly hosts, we sing a hymn to Thy glory, saying without ceasing:

• *Sanctus, page 45.*

COMMUNION: 4 Esdras 2:35, 34. May eternal light shine upon them, O Lord, with Thy saints forever, because Thou art merciful. **V.** Eternal rest grant unto them, O Lord, and let perpetual light shine upon them, with thy saints forever, because Thou art merciful.

POSTCOMMUNION: May the prayer of Thy suppliants profit the souls of Thy servants and handmaids, we beseech Thee, O Lord, that Thou may free them from all sins and make them sharers in Thy redemption. Who live and reign with God the Father, in the unity of the Holy Spirit, God, world without end. Amen.

• *Concluding prayers, page 75.*

COMMON OF THE BLESSED VIRGIN MARY

(NB: Prayers and Readings are taken from the 1962 Missal)

• *Beginning of the Mass, page 19.*

Introit: Hail, holy Mother, who in childbirth brought forth the King Who rules heaven and earth for ever and ever. (*P. T.* Alleluia, alleluia.) *Ps.* 44:2. My heart has uttered a good word; I speak my works to the King. V. Glory be...

• *Kyrie and Gloria, page 27.*

Prayer: Grant to us, Thy servants, O Lord God, we beseech Thee, to enjoy continual health of mind and body, and, by the glorious intercession of Blessed Mary ever Virgin, to be delivered from present sorrow and partake of the fullness of eternal joy. Through our Lord...

Epistle: Ecclesiasticus 24:14-16. From the beginning, and before the world, was I created, and unto the world to come I shall not cease to be, and in the holy dwelling place I have ministered before Him. And so was I established in Sion, and in the holy city likewise I rested, and my power was in Jerusalem. And I took root in an honorable people, and in the portion of my God His inheritance, and my abode is in the full assembly of saints.

Gradual: Blessed and venerable art thou, O Virgin Mary, who with unsullied virginity was found to be the Mother of our Savior. **V.** O Virgin Mother of God, He whom the whole world cannot contain, becoming man, enclosed Himself in thy womb.

Alleluia, alleluia. **V.** After childbirth you still remained an inviolate Virgin; Mother of God, intercede for us. Alleluia.

In Advent, omit the Alleluia *and the Verse and instead pray:*

Alleluia, alleluia. **V**. Luke 1:28. Hail Mary, full of grace; the Lord is with thee; blessed art thou among women. Alleluia.

After Septuagesima omit the Alleluia *and the Verse and instead pray:*

Tract: Rejoice, O Virgin Mary, for thou alone has put an end to all heresies. **V.** Thou who believed the words of the Archangel Gabriel. **V.** Still a virgin, thou did bring forth God and man, and after childbirth thou did remain an inviolate virgin. **V.** Mother of God, intercede for us.

During the Paschaltime, the Gradual is replaced by the following:

Alleluia, alleluia. **V.** Numbers 17:8. The rod of Jesse has blossomed; a Virgin has conceived Him Who is both God and man. God has given back peace to the earth, reconciling in Himself the lowliness of earth to the majesty of heaven. Alleluia. **V.** Luke 1:28. Hail Mary, full of grace; the Lord is with thee: blessed art thou amongst women. Alleluia.

- *Prayer: Cleanse My Heart, page 31.*

Gospel: Luke 11:27-28. At that time, as Jesus was speaking to the multitudes, a certain woman from the crowd, lifting up her voice, said to Him: "Blessed is the womb that bore Thee and the breasts that gave Thee suck." But He said: "Yea rather, blessed are they who hear the word of God and keep it."

Offertory: Luke 1:28, 42. Hail Mary, full of grace; the Lord is with thee: blessed art thou among women, and blessed is the fruit of thy womb. (*P. T.* Alleluia.)

• *Offertory Prayers, page 37.*

Secret: By Thy gracious mercy, O Lord, and the intercession of Blessed Mary ever Virgin, may this oblation profit us for peace and well being now and for evermore. Through our Lord...

PREFACE OF THE BLESSED VIRGIN MARY

It is truly meet and just, right and helpful for our salvation, that we should at all times and in all places give thanks to Thee, O holy Lord, Father almighty, everlasting God: and on the Festivity of the Blessed Mary, ever a Virgin, should praise and bless and proclaim Thee. For she conceived Thy only-begotten Son by the overshadowing of the Holy Spirit, and losing not the glory of her virginity, gave to the world the everlasting Light, Jesus Christ our Lord. Through whom the Angels praise Thy Majesty, the Dominions worship it, and the Powers stand in awe. The Heavens and the heavenly hosts and the blessed Seraphim join together in celebrating their joy. With these we pray Thee join our own voices also, while we say with lowly praise:

• *Sanctus, page 45.*

Communion: Blessed is the womb of the Virgin Mary, which bore the Son of the Eternal Father. (*P. T.* Alleluia.)

Postcommunion: Having received the aids of our everlasting salvation, O Lord, we beseech Thee, grant us to be everywhere protected by the patronage of Blessed Mary ever Virgin, in veneration of whom we have made these offerings to Thy Majesty. Through our Lord...

• *Concluding prayers, page 75.*

A FINAL WORD

And the Word was made flesh, and dwelt among us.
—JOHN 1:14 *(Douay Rheims)*

In 2007, Pope Benedict XVI granted greater freedom to celebrate the traditional Latin Mass in the express hope that it would be mutually enriching, since the exclusion of either form would not be consistent with the recognition of their "value and holiness." He hoped the reverent celebration of the Latin Mass would spiritually nourish the faithful, and would introduce many to a "new" form of the liturgy, our public worship. In turn, this experience could deepen our reverence at the Ordinary form—the "Novus Ordo" Mass commonly celebrated today—and help us to experience Christ present in a more complete and profound manner.

In the end, liturgy is something God does for *us*, through His Son Christ Jesus, the Light of the world. We respond in humility and gratitude to His true and Real Presence. We learn from our Mother Mary, who heard God's invitation, received His Word, and responded in faith—without understanding completely—how to best worship God and to follow her Son.

All that leads to true communion with God is authentic; all that impedes it is not. Let us, then, open wide our hearts, and step out in faith to worship God at the Latin Mass, "to the praise and glory of His name, and to the benefit of all His Holy Church, our beloved family of faith." Ad Majorem Dei Gloriam! Amen.